# Could We
# Be Friends?

## POEMS FOR PALS

❖❖❖❖❖❖❖❖❖❖

### BY BOBBI KATZ

### PICTURES BY JOUNG UN KIM

École Lochiel

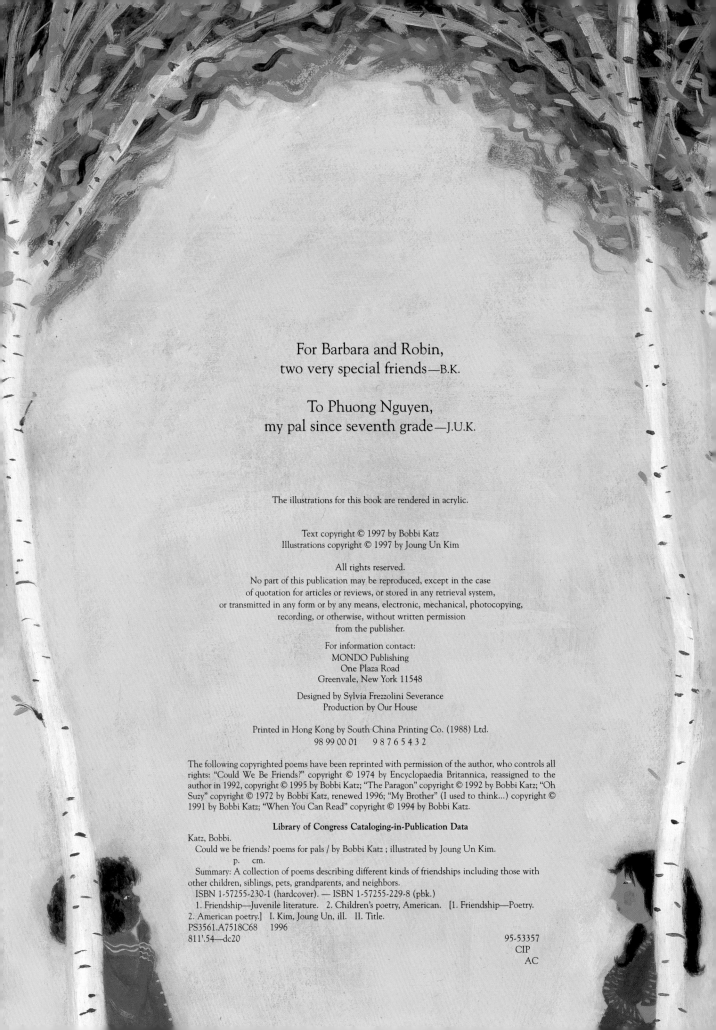

For Barbara and Robin,
two very special friends—B.K.

To Phuong Nguyen,
my pal since seventh grade—J.U.K.

The illustrations for this book are rendered in acrylic.

Text copyright © 1997 by Bobbi Katz
Illustrations copyright © 1997 by Joung Un Kim

For information contact:
MONDO Publishing
One Plaza Road
Greenvale, New York 11548

Designed by Sylvia Frezzolini Severance
Production by Our House

Printed in Hong Kong by South China Printing Co. (1988) Ltd.
98 99 00 01    9 8 7 6 5 4 3 2

The following copyrighted poems have been reprinted with permission of the author, who controls all
rights: "Could We Be Friends?" copyright © 1974 by Encyclopaedia Britannica, reassigned to the
author in 1992, copyright © 1995 by Bobbi Katz; "The Paragon" copyright © 1992 by Bobbi Katz; "Oh
Suzy" copyright © 1972 by Bobbi Katz, renewed 1996; "My Brother" (I used to think...) copyright ©
1991 by Bobbi Katz; "When You Can Read" copyright © 1994 by Bobbi Katz.

**Library of Congress Cataloging-in-Publication Data**
Katz, Bobbi.
  Could we be friends? poems for pals / by Bobbi Katz ; illustrated by Joung Un Kim.
      p.    cm.
  Summary: A collection of poems describing different kinds of friendships including those with
other children, siblings, pets, grandparents, and neighbors.
  ISBN 1-57255-230-1 (hardcover). — ISBN 1-57255-229-8 (pbk.)
  1. Friendship—Juvenile literature.  2. Children's poetry, American.  [1. Friendship—Poetry.
2. American poetry.]  I. Kim, Joung Un, ill.  II. Title.
PS3561.A7518C68    1996
811'.54—dc20                                                                                    95-53357
                                                                                                CIP
                                                                                                AC

# CONTENTS

## Kids

Some of us have black hair.
Some have blond or brown.
Some of us are city kids.
Some live in a small town.
Some of us ride buses.
Some walk to school each day.
Some of us like studying.
Some only want to play.
Some of us are quiet kids.
Some love making noise.
We're every color, shape, and size.
We're girls and we are boys.
Some are learning English.
And that's quite hard to do.
(What makes it even harder,
is if kids laugh at you.)

We're different in so many ways.
The list could get so long.
But think of how we are alike,
and that list won't be wrong:
All of us are children.
All of us like fun.
All of us are special—
every single one.
All of us share just one home.
It's called the planet, Earth.
All of us are dreamers . . .
and all our dreams have worth.

## Could We Be Friends?

I wonder what your name is.
I wonder who you are—
Kid making faces
        from the back seat
             of a car.

When you stick your tongue out,
                    I stick mine out, too.
When you smile and wave at me,
                    I wave back at you!
I wonder where your house is—
What games you like to play.
But when the traffic light turns green,
my father drives away.

## Chris

Bike rider—
Hike taker—
Inventor of games—
Keeper of secrets—
Sharer of jokes—
We toss thoughts
back and forth
the way we play catch.
Back and forth—

Back and forth—
our goofiest thoughts are safe
with each other.
I wouldn't trade you for a brother.
With you there is no pretend.
Me and you—a team of two—
Chris, my friend.

## The Paragon

Yuk! How I hate Nancy Feder!
Why, oh why, does the world need her?
Since Nancy Feder moved next door,
life's not worth living anymore.
I don't know how my mother knows
she makes her bed and folds her clothes
and does her homework everyday
before she goes outside to play.
She's such a goodie, goodie, good—
she'd make you barf! I bet she would!
(And you don't have to listen to
my mother rave the way I do!)
A rabbit's foot might bring me luck,
and then I'll see a moving truck.
Won't it be a sunny day,
when Nancy Feder moves away?

## Oh, Suzy

Oh, Suzy,
roughy-toughy-Suzy-friend.
Why did you move away?
Other girls do stupid stuff
like playing dumb old house
and dressing up their creepy dolls.
No one wants to wrestle
or roll down hills—
    over
      and
        over—
          so
            many
              overs.
Oh, Suzy,
roughy-toughy-Suzy-friend.
Why did you move away?

## New Neighbors

A family's moving into the house
across the street, I see.
A Mom, a Dad, and three weird kids—
One might be the same age as me.
His sister is too little.
His brother is too tall.
That middle kid might be in my class.
I'm sure I won't like him at all.
Oh no, he's coming up our stairs.
He's ringing our front bell.
I know that I won't like him.
Already I can tell.

*Well yes. I'm glad to meet you, too.*
*Do I trade baseball cards? I do.*
*You'll be in Mrs. Warren's class.*
*Yes, she gives tests. Keep cool. You'll pass.*
*I'll show you around the neighborhood.*
*Tomorrow morning? That sounds good.*

A family moved into the house
across the street today.
José, their kid, will be my friend.
I knew it right away.

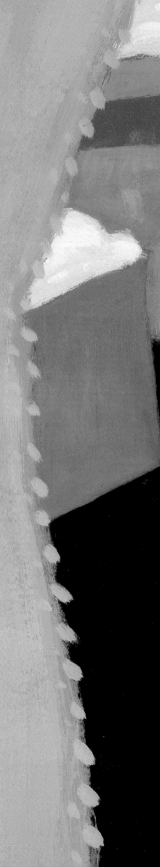

## First Day, New School

Someone showed me where to go.
Someone smiled and said, "Hello."
Someone said, "There's room. Sit here."
    And
something started to disappear:
    Little
    by little
    it
    became
    so
    small—
    that scared hole
    in my heart's
    hardly there
    at all.

## Words

*Sticks and stones*
*will break my bones.*
*But words will never hurt me.*

Gramps told me these words are true.
He learned them long ago.
Gramps always seems to get stuff right.
This time, I just don't know.

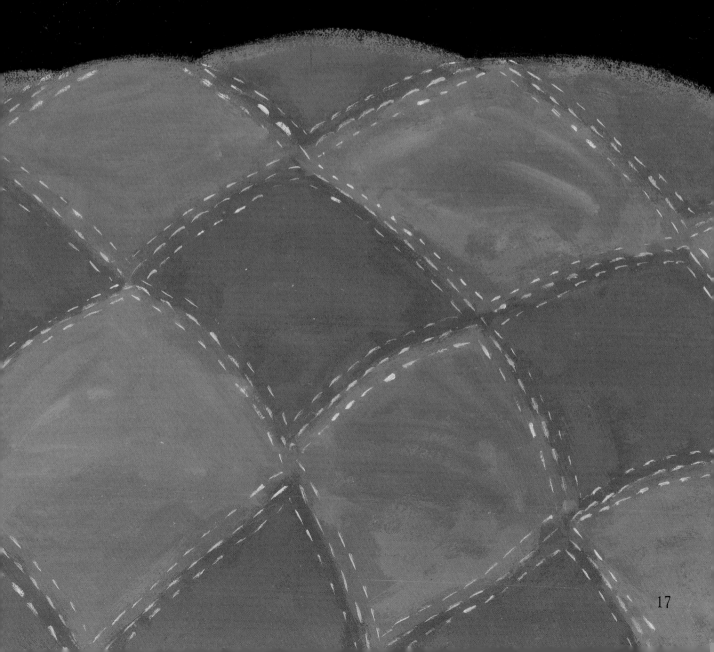

They called me a name,
and I walked right by.
I didn't start a fight.
But the word they said
is a stick in my head
and a stone in my bed . . .
all night.

## My Sister

I remember the day
we brought you home
from the hospital—
so small and useless.
Some "new playmate!"

## My Brother

Sometimes you're almost my friend,
but mostly you're my enemy.
From zero to one hundred,
I like you zero minus.

## My Sister

Sometimes when you
fall asleep,
curled close like a kitten
in the back seat of the car,
I forget I hate you.

## My Brother

I used to think
how good it would be
if I was the onliest
kid in this house.
But when you went to camp,
I was the loneliest.

## A Birthday Wish

When I blew out the candles
on my birthday cake,
the wish I made was different
than the wish I planned to make.
I looked at the circle of candles,
and each of them was glowing.
I took a breath and closed my eyes.
The circle started changing and growing!

Each candle turned into a kid,
and those kids were holding hands.
The circle looped around the globe
with kids from many lands.
My friends began to holler, "Blow!"
So I started blowing. And . . .
I
wished
for a circle
with no kids left out—
growing and growing and growing!

# Granny's Autograph Book

One day I found a dark blue book
with a strange and special look.
Bumpy leather, trimmed with gold—
I knew that it was very old.
A witch's book with a magic spell?
Granny would know and she would tell.

*"Messages on pastel pages . . .*
*My autograph book! I've kept it for ages.*
*Magic spells? Yes, of a kind.*
*Look inside. See what you find."*

Granny unlocked it with a key.
Then she handed her book to me.
Pale green, pale yellow, blue, and pink—
page after page with words in ink.
On each page was a saying or a rhyme,
signed by a friend from another time.
One page was signed by the class clown,
who drew his picture upside down.
The book cast a magic spell, it's true.
Granny's friends became *real* kids
            like me . . .
                  and you!

# The Empty Lot: A Modern Fairy Tale

A useless space with layers of litter—
A disgrace of a place. My life was bitter.
One day an old man took pity on me.
He saw how different I could be.
By himself with a shovel and hoe,
he planted a tree that began to grow.
First one by one, then two by two,
strangers turned into a friendly crew.
They hauled away the piles of junk—
old tires, glass, a rusty trunk.
They dug and raked and brought in soil
and made a garden with their toil!

Now new friends trade tools and swap stories,
among my begonias and blue morning glories.
Tomatoes, daisies, petunias, and roses
sip cool drinks through bright green hoses.
People even visit from *other* blocks
to see my sweet peas and hollyhocks!
They're ALL at the ball, and my life is sweet.
I'm the Cinderella of Sullivan Street.

> And *happily, forever after,*
> *the lot was a place of peace and laughter.*

## Cat Speak

"Here, kitty, kitty!"
Imagine that!
Where did *they* learn to speak to a cat?
Annoying me while I'm taking my ease
in my blue comfy chair in the sun,
if you please.
Annoying me when I'm taking a nap!
Picking me up to plop on a lap!
They have things in a terrible muddle.
*I'll* decide with whom I'll cuddle.
Perhaps I'll let them stroke my fur,
and when *I* wish, perhaps I'll purr.
Perhaps I'll brush against a leg.
But I give the orders, and *I* don't beg.

## My Girl

They locked me in the city pound,
but you should see the girl I found!
I took one look, one careful smell.
I knew that things would work out well!

She's cute and gentle—smart and sweet.
She gave me a *real* name. It's Pete.

She likes Frisbee, so I play.
(I mostly let her have her way.)
And I will "sit" and "fetch" and "stay"—
And love her . . .
        to my dying day.

## Chicken Pox

My brother caught the chicken pox—
the dotty, spotty chicken pox.
My brother caught the chicken pox—
and now I've got spots, too.

Our parents say that we must learn
to share our things and wait our turn.
They say that life is "give and take,"
but parents might make a mistake.
Look how my brother learned to share!
He gave. I took. Now we're a pair.

My brother caught the chicken pox—
the itchy, scritchy chicken pox.
My brother caught the chicken pox—
and now I've got spots, too.

## Medicine

Doctors!  Doctors!
What do they say?
"Medicine! Medicine!
Four times a day."

I wouldn't make a snake
take the glop that I take!
I must "rest" in my bed.
All my books have been read.
All my puzzles are done.
Being sick isn't fun.
I am bored with TV.
I am bored being ME!

Pictures! Pictures!
They came at half-past three.
All the kids in my class
drew pictures for ME.
Doctors! Doctors!
They'll say, "It can't be true."
But I'm getting better
from the pictures my pals drew.

Dear Gina,
Vacation is terrific.
We go to the beach each day.
I'm bringing you all the best sea shells.
I hope your sick gerbil's okay.

p.s. Please write

Me

Dear Gramps,
I wish you were here to go fishing
from the shore or a boat in the bay.
I ate steamed clams for you
like you asked me to do.
They're just as good as you say.

p.s. Please write

Me

Dear Grandma,
The waves are ice-cold and enormous.
I dive and I splash and I jump.
I built you a beautiful castle.
Then the tide turned it into a lump.

p.s.  Please write

Me

Dear Patrick—
I met a kid who looks like you,
except he's not as tall
and his eyes aren't blue
and he doesn't like doing
the same things we do.
I play with him, and I miss . . . YOU.

Me

p.s.  Please write

## When You Can Read

When you can read, then you can go
from Kalamazoo to Idaho—
Or read directions that explain
just how to build a model plane—
Or bake a cake or cook a stew—
The words will tell you what to do!
When you can read, then you can play
a brand new game the proper way—
Or get a letter from a friend
and read it . . . to the very end.